This article has really filled in the "voids" that kept me from fully understanding things. I have found it to be one of the best discussions on the subject of freedom, and how our own Government has managed to take that freedom away from us, all the while giving lip service to the Constitution. The title of this article is **"The UCC Connection"**. The noteworthy author is Howard Freeman. It is dated September 22, 1991.

THE UCC CONNECTION - How To Free Yourself From Legal Tyranny

by Howard Freeman

<u>FORWARD</u>

This is a slightly condensed, casually paraphrased transcript of tapes of a seminar given by Howard Freeman in 1990. It was prepared to make available Mr. Freeman's knowledge and experience in his search for an accessible and understandable explanation of the confusing state of the government and the courts. It should be helpful to those who want to develop a deeper understanding of this information without having to listen to three or four hours of recorded material.

The **frustrations** many Americans feel about our judicial system can be overwhelming, and often frightening; and like most fear, it is based on the lack of understanding or knowledge. Those of us who have chosen a path out of bondage and into liberty are faced, eventually, with the **seemingly tyrannical power** of some governmental agency and the **mystifying and awesome power** of the courts. We have been taught that we must "get a good lawyer", but that is becoming increasingly difficult, if not impossible. If we are defending ourselves from the government, we find that the lawyers quickly take our money and then tell us as the ship is sinking, "I can't help you with that — I'm an officer of the court."

Ultimately, the only way for us to ever have a "snowballs' chance" is to understand the **RULES OF THE GAME** and to come to and understanding of the true nature of the Law. The lawyers have established and secured a virtual monopoly over this area of human knowledge by implying that the subject is just too difficult for the **AVERAGE PERSON** to understand; and by creating a separate vocabulary out of English words of otherwise common usage. While it may at times seem hopelessly complicated, it is not that difficult to grasp; are lawyers really as smart as they would have us believe?

Besides, anyone who has been through a legal battle against the government with the aid of a lawyer has come to realize that **lawyers know procedure**, not law.

*"Then answered one of the lawyers, and said unto him, Master, **thus saying** thou reproachest us also. And he said, **Woe unto you also, ye lawyers!** for ye lade men with burdens grievous to be borne, and ye yourselves touch not the burdens with one of your fingers... **Woe unto you, lawyers!** for ye have taken away **the key of knowledge**: ye entered not in yourselves, and them that were entering in ye hindered."* (Christ teaches his disciples; at Luke 11:45-52).

Besides... Anyone who has been through a legal battle against the government with the aid of a lawyer has come to realize that **lawyers learn about procedure**, not about law.

Mr. Freeman admits that he is not a lawyer, and as such, he has a way of explaining law to us that puts it well within our reach.

Consider also that **the Framers of the Constitution** wrote in language simple enough that the people could understand, specifically so that it would **NOT** have to be interpreted.

So again we find, as in many other areas of life, **"THE BUCK STOPS HERE!"**

It is **WE** who must take the responsibility for finding and putting to good use the **TRUTH!** It is WE who must claim and defend our God given Rights and our Freedom from those who would take them from us. It is **WE** who must protect ourselves, our families, and our posterity from the inevitable intrusion into our lives by those who live parasitically off the labor, skill and talents of others.

To these ends, Mr. Freeman offers a simple, hopeful explanation of our plight and a **PEACEFUL** method of dealing with it. Please take note that this lecture represents one chapter in the book of his understanding, which he is always refining, expanding, improving. It is, as all bits of wisdom are, a point of departure from which to begin our own **journey into understanding**, so that we all might be able to pass on to others: **greater knowledge and hope**, and to God: the gift of lives lived in peace, freedom and praise.

"I send you forth as sheep in the midst of wolves, be ye therefore wise as serpents, and harmless as doves." (Matthew 10:16).

INTRODUCTION

When I beat the IRS, I used Supreme Court (SC) decisions. If I had tried to use these in court, I would have been convicted.

I was involved with a patriot group and I studied Supreme Court cases. I concluded that the SC had declared that I was not a person required to file an income tax — that that tax was **an excise tax on privileges** granted by government.

So I quit filing and paying income taxes and it was not long before they came down on me with a heavy hand. They issued a **Notice of Deficiency**, which had such a fantastic sum on it that the biggest temptation was to go in with their letter and say "Where in the world did you ever get that figure?" They claimed I owed them some $60,000! But even if I *had* been paying taxes, I never in the world had that much money, so how could I have owed them that much?

SECTION 1: Never Argue The Amount Of Deficiency.

Fortunately, I had been given just a little bit of information: **NEVER ARGUE THE FACTS IN A TAX CASE.** [MAXIM: "ARGUMENTS ARE FOR FOOLS"]. If you're not required to file, what do you care whether they say you owe sixty dollars or $60,000 dollars. If you are not required to file, the amount doesn't matter. **DON'T ARGUE THE AMOUNT** — that is an issue of fact.

In most instances, when you get a **Notice of Deficiency**, it is usually for some fantastic amount. The minute you say, "I don't owe that much," you have voluntarily agreed that you owe them something, and you have just given them jurisdiction.

Just don't be shocked at the amount on a **Notice of Deficiency**, (NOD) even if it's ten million dollars! If the law says that you are not required to file or pay tax, the amount doesn't matter.

By arguing the amount, they will just say that you must go to tax court and decide what the amount is to be. By the time you get to tax court, the law issues are all decided. You are only there to decide **HOW MUCH YOU OWE**. They will not listen to arguments of law.

So I went to see the agent and told him that I wasn't required to file. He said, "You **ARE** required to file, Mr. Freeman." But I had all these SC cases, and I started reading them to him.

He said, "I don't know anything about law, Mr. Freeman, but the Code says that **you are required to file**, and you're going to pay that amount or you're going to go to tax court." I thought that someone there ought to know something about law, so I asked to talk to his superior. I went to him and got out my SC cases, and he wouldn't listen to them. "I don't know anything about law, Mr. Freeman..." Finally I got to the **Problems Resolution Officer**, and he said the same thing. He said that the only person above him was the **District Director**.

So I went to see him. By the time I got to his office, they had phoned ahead, and his secretary said he was out. But I heard someone in his office, and I knew he was there.

I went down the elevator, around the corner to the Federal Building and into Senator Simpson's office. There was a girl sitting there at a desk, and she asked me if she could help me. I told her my problem. I said that I really think the District Director is up there. I asked her to call the IRS and tell them that it was Senator Simpson's office calling and to ask if the District Director is in. I said, "If you get him on the phone, tell him that you are from the Senator's office and you have a person whom you are sending over to speak to him — if he is, can he wait just five minutes." It worked.

He was there, so I ran back up to his office. His secretary met me when I came in and said, "Mr. Freeman, you're so lucky — the Director just arrived."

The Director was very nice and offered me coffee and cookies and we sat and talked. So he asked me what I wanted to talk to him about. (If you've never have someone say to you, "I'm from the government and I'm here to help you", watch out! — But we can turn that around and approach them in the same way). So I said, "I thought you ought to know that there are agents working for you who are writing letters over your name that you wouldn't agree with. Do you read all the mail that goes out of this office over your signature?" The Director said, "Oh, I couldn't read everything — it goes out here by the bag full." (That was what I thought). I said, "There are some of your agents writing letters which contradict the decisions of the Supreme Court of the

United States and they're not doing it over **THEIR** name, they're doing it over **YOUR** name."

He was very interested to hear about it and asked if I had any examples. I just happened to have some with me, so I got them out and presented them to him. [Supreme Court cases supporting Freeman's position].

The Director thought it was very interesting and asked if I could leave this information with him, which I did. He said he would look it over and contact me within 3 days. Three days later he called me up and said, "I'm sure, Mr. Freeman, that you will be glad to know that your Notice of Deficiency has been withdrawn. We've determined that you're not a person required to file. Your file is closed and you will hear no more from us." I haven't heard another word from them since. That was in 1980, and I haven't filed since 1969.

SECTION 2: The Supreme Court On Trial.

I thought sure I had the answer, but when a friend got charged with Willful Failure to File an income tax, he asked me to help him. I told him that they would have to prove that he **willfully** failed to file and I suggested that he should put me on the witness stand. He should ask me if I spoke at a certain time and place in Scott's Bluff, and did I see him in the audience. He should then ask me what I spoke about that day.

When I got on the stand. I brought out all of the SC cases I had used with the District Director. I thought I would be lucky to get a sentence or two out before the judge cut me off, but I was reading whole paragraphs and the judge didn't stop me.

I read one and then another and so on. And finally when I had read just about as much as I thought I should, the judge called a recess of the court. I told Bob I thought we had it made. There was just no way that they could rule against him after all that testimony. So we relaxed.

The prosecution presented it's case and he [Bob] decided to rest his case on my testimony, which showed that he was not required to file and that the SC had upheld this position.

The prosecutor then presented his closing statements, and we were just sure that he had won. But at the very end, the judge spoke to the jury and told them, "You will decide **the facts of this case** and I will give you **the law**. The law required this man to file and income tax form; you decide whether or not he filed it." What a shock! The jury convicted him. Later some of the members of the jury said, "What could we do? The man had admitted that he had not filed the form, so we had to convict him."

As soon as the trial was over, I went around to the judge's office and he was just coming in through his back door. I said, "Judge, by what authority do you overturn the standing decisions of the United States SC? You sat on the bench while I read that case law. Now how do you, a District Court Judge, have the authority to overturn decisions of the Supreme Court?"

He says, "Oh, those were old decisions." I said, "Those are standing decisions. They have never been overturned. I don't care how old they are; you have no right to overturn a standing decision of the US SC in a District Court."

SECTION 3: Public Law v. Public Policy.

He said, "Name any decision of the Supreme Court after 1938 and I'll honor it, but all the decisions you read were prior to 1938. He went on, "Prior to 1938, the Supreme Court was dealing with **Public Law**; since 1938, the Supreme Court has dealt with **Public Policy**. The charge that Mr. S. was being tried for is a **Public Policy Statute**; not **Public Public Law**, and those Supreme Court cases do not apply to Public Policy." I asked him what happened in 1938. He said that he had already told me too much — he wasn't going to tell me any more.

SECTION 4: 1938 And The Erie Railroad.

Well, I began to investigate. I found that 1938 was the year of the **Erie Railroad v. Tompkins** case of the Supreme Court. It was also the year the courts claim they **blended Law with Equity**. I read the Erie Railroad case. A man had sued the Erie railroad for damages when he was struck by a board sticking out of a boxcar as he walked along beside the tracks. The district court had decided on **Commercial Law** (Negotiable Instruments Law); that this man was not under any **contract** with the Erie Railroad, and therefore **he lacked standing** to sue the company. Under **Common Law** (Natural Law) he was damaged and he would have had the right to sue.

This overturned a standing decision of over one hundred years.

Swift v. Tyson in 1840 was a similar case, and the decision of the Supreme Court then was that in a case of this type, the court would judge by the **Common Law** (Natural Law) of the State where the incident occurred - in this case, Pennsylvania. In the Erie Railroad case, the Supreme Court now ruled that all federal cases will be judged under the **Negotiable Instruments Law**. There would be no more decisions based on the Common Law at the federal level. So here we find the **blending of Law with Equity**.

This was a puzzle to me. As I put these new pieces together I reasoned that all our courts since 1938 were **Merchant Law courts** and not **Common Law courts**. There were still pieces missing from the puzzle.

SECTION 5: A Friend In Court.

Fortunately, I made a friend of a judge. Now you won't make friends with a judge if you go into the court like a "wolf in black sheep country." You must approach him as though you are the sheep and he is the wolf. If you go into court as a wolf, if you make demands and tell the judge what the law is — how he had better uphold the law or else. Remember the verse: *"I send you forth as sheep in the midst of wolves, be ye therefore wise as serpents, and harmless as doves."* We have to go into court and be **wise and harmless**, and not make demands. We must **be humble (and play a little dumb)** and ask a lot of questions. Well, I asked a lot of questions and boxed the judges into a corner where they had to give me a victory or admit what they didn't want to admit.

I won the next case and on the way out I had to stop by the clerk's office to get some papers. One of the judges stopped and said, "You're an interesting man, Mr. Freeman. If you're ever in town, stop by and if I'm not sitting on a case we will visit."

SECTION 6: America Is Bankrupt.

Later, when I went to visit the judge, I told him of my problem with the Supreme Court cases dealing with **Public Policy** rather than **Public Law**. He said, "In 1938, all the higher judges, the top attorneys, and the U.S. Attorneys were called into a secret meeting and this is what we were told: **"America is a bankrupt nation. It is owned completely by its creditors.** The creditors own Congress, they own the Executive, they own the Judiciary and they own all the State Governments. Take silent judicial notice of this fact, but never reveal it openly."

"Your court is operating under **Admiralty Jurisdiction** - call it anything you want, but do not call it Admiralty."

SECTION 7: Admiralty Courts.

The reason they cannot call it Admiralty Jurisdiction is that your defense would be quite different in Admiralty Jurisdiction from your defense under the Common Law. In **Admiralty**, no court has jurisdiction unless there is a **valid International contract** in dispute. When you know it is Admiralty Jurisdiction, and they have admitted on the record that you are in an Admiralty Court, you can demand that the **international maritime contract**, to which you are supposedly party, and which you supposedly have breached, be placed into evidence.

No court has **Admiralty/Maritime Jurisdiction** unless there is a valid international maritime contract that has been breached.

So you say, just innocently like a lamb, "Well, I never knew that I got involved with an international maritime contract, so I deny that such a contract exists. If this court is taking jurisdiction in Admiralty, then place the contract into evidence, so that I might challenge the validity of the contract." What they would have to do is place the **national debt** into evidence. They would have to admit that **the international bankers own the whole nation, and that we are the banker's slaves**.

<u>**SECTION 8:**</u> Not Expedient.

But the bankers said it is not expedient **at this time** to admit that **they own everything and could foreclose on every nation of the world**.

[This is the **KEY** behind the build up of the United Nations as a **MILITARY FORCE**! This is the **KEY** to disarming America. This is the **KEY** to ending the cold war. Like now we have no more enemy, so we can melt all our guns. **WRONG!** The bankers **plan to foreclose**, they just don't want **THEIR HEADS BLOWN OFF WHILE DOING IT**, so they **dictate to Congress** to get rid of the guns, etc.]

The reason they don't want to tell everyone that they own everything is that **there are still too many privately owned guns in America today**. There are uncooperative armies and other military forces. So until they can gradually **consolidate all armies** into a **WORLD ARMY**, and all courts into a **WORLD COURT**, it is not expedient to admit the **jurisdiction of the courts** they are operating under.

When we understand these things, we realize that there are certain secrets they don't want to admit, and we can use this to our benefit.

SECTION 9: Jurisdiction.

The Constitution of the United States mentions three areas of jurisdiction in which the courts may operate:

SECTION 10: Common Law.

Common Law (Natural or Constitutional Law) is based on our Creator's Laws as originally presented by Moses. Anytime someone is charged under the Common Law, there must be a damaged party. You are free under the Common Law to do anything you pleases, as long as you do not infringe on the life, liberty, or property of someone else. You have a right to make a fool of yourself provided you do not infringe on the life, liberty, or property of someone else. The Common Law does not allow for any government action which prevents a man from making a fool of himself. For instance, when you the cross state line, you will probably see a sign which says, "BUCKLE YOUR SEAT BELTS - IT'S THE LAW." This cannot be Common Law because who would you injure if you did not buckle up? **Nobody.**

This would be **compelled performance**. But Common Law cannot compel performance. Any violation of Common Law is a **CRIMINAL ACT** that is punishable.

SECTION 11: Equity Law.

Equity Law is law which **compels performance**. It compels you to perform to the **exact letter of any contract** that you are under. So, if you have **compelled performance**, there must be a contract somewhere and you are being compelled to perform under the **obligation** of the contract. Now this can only be a **civil action** — not criminal. In **Equity Jurisdiction**, you cannot be tried criminally, but you can be **compelled to perform** to the letter of the contract. If you then refuse to perform as directed by the court, you can be charged with **contempt of court**, this is a **criminal action**. Are our set belt laws Equity laws? No. They are not, because you cannot be penalized or punished under Equity jurisdiction for not keeping to the letter of a contract. [This has of course changed since the publishing of this article; so read on].

SECTION 12: Admiralty or Maritime Law.

Admiralty is a civil jurisdiction of **Compelled Performance**, which has **Criminal Penalties** for not adhering to the letter of a contract, but this only applies to **international contracts**.

Now we can see what jurisdiction the seat belt laws (and all traffic laws, building codes, ordinances, tax codes, etc.) are under. Whenever there is a penalty for **failure to perform** (such as willful failure to file) that is **Admiralty/Maritime Law** and there must be a valid international contract in force.

However, the courts don't want to admit that they are operating under **Admiralty/Maritime Jurisdiction** [hereafter noted as **A/M**], so they took the international law or Law Merchant and adopted it into our codes. This is what the SC decided in the Erie Railroad case - that the decisions would be based on commercial law (or business law) and that there will be criminal penalties associated with it. Since judges were instructed to not call it **A/M** Jurisdiction, they call it **Statutory Jurisdiction**.

[I looked for Statutory Jurisdiction in the 4th edition of Black's Law Dictionary. It's not there, so I looked up Statute, and under its definition is this paragraph: This word is used to designate the

written law in contradistinction to the **unwritten law**. *Foster v. Brown,* 199 Ga. 444, 34 S.E.2d, 530 535 See Common Law.]

[Unwritten law is common law; "contradistinction" means "as opposed to" "opposite to."]

SECTION 13: Courts Of Contract.

You may ask how we got into this situation where we can be charged with failure to wear set belts and be fined for it. Isn't the judge sworn to up hold the Constitution? Yes. But you must understand that in **Art. I, Sect. 10**, the Constitution gives us the **unlimited right to contract** as long as we do not infringe on the life, liberty, or property of someone else. **Contracts are enforceable**, and the Constitution gives two jurisdictions where contracts can be enforced, **Equity or Admiralty**. But we find them being enforced in **Statutory Jurisdiction**. This is an embarrassing part for the courts that we can use to box the judges into a corner in their own courts. We will cover this more later.

SECTION 14: Contracts Must Be Voluntary.

Under the Common Law, both parties must enter into every contract **knowingly, voluntarily, and intentionally** or the contract is unenforceable and void. These are characteristics of a **Common Law contract**.

There is another characteristic - **the contract must be based on substance**. For example, contracts used to read, "For one dollar and other valuable consideration, I will paint your house, etc." That was a valid contract — the dollar was a genuine silver dollar.

Now suppose you wrote a contract that said, "For one Federal Reserve Note (FRN) and other considerations, I will paint your house." And suppose, for example, I painted your house the wrong color. Could you go into a Common Law court and get justice? NO, you could not. No substance, no contract.

You see, a Federal Reserve Note is a "colorable" dollar as it has no substance, and in a **Common Law jurisdiction** that contract would be unenforceable.

"Colorable: That which is in appearance only, and not what it purports to be; hence counterfeit, feigned, having the appearance of truth." (Black's Law Dictionary, 5th ed.)

SECTION 15: Colorable Money And Colorable Courts.

The word "colorable" means **something that appears to be genuine, but is not**.

Maybe it looks like a dollar, and maybe it spends like a dollar, but it if is not **redeemable for lawful money (silver or gold)** it is "colorable"; fiat; fake; false. If a Federal Reserve Note is used in a contract, then the contract becomes a "colorable" contract. And "colorable" contracts can only be enforced under a "colorable" jurisdiction. So by creating Federal Reserve Notes, the government had to create a "colorable" jurisdiction to cover the kinds of contracts that use them. We now have what is called **Statutory Jurisdiction**, which is not a genuine **Admiralty jurisdiction**. Judges are enforcing a "colorable" Admiralty Jurisdiction because we are using **"colorable money"**. **Colorable Admiralty** is now known as **Statutory Jurisdiction**. So let's see how we got under this Statutory Jurisdiction.

SECTION 16: Uniform Commercial Code.

The government established a **"colorable" law system** to fit their **"Colorable" currency**.

It used to be called the **Law Merchant** or the **Law of Redeemable Instruments** because it dealt with paper, which was redeemable in something of substance. But once Federal Reserve Notes had been **declared unredeemable**, there had to be a system of law which was **completely "colorable"** from start to finish. This system of law is codified as the Uniform Commercial Code (UCC), and has been adopted in every state of the Union. This is **"colorable" law**, used in all of the courts of the nation.

I explained one of the keys earlier, which is that **the country is bankrupt and we have no rights**. If the master says "Jump" the slave had better jump, because the master has the right to cut off his head. **As slaves we have no rights.** But the **Creditors/ Masters** had to cover up that fact, so they created the system of law called the UCC. This **"colorable" jurisdiction** under the UCC is the next Key to understanding what has happened.

SECTION 17: Contract Or Agreement.

One difference between **Common Law** and the **UCC** is that in Common Law, contracts must be entered into: (1) knowingly, (2) voluntarily, and (3) intentionally. Under the UCC this is not so. First of all, **contracts are necessary**, but under the UCC, **"agreements"** can be binding, and if you only exercise the benefits of an **"agreement"** it is presumed, or implied, that you intend to meet the **obligations** associated with the those **benefits**. If you accept a benefit offered by government, you are **obligated** to follow every statute involved with that **benefit.**

So **their method** is to get everybody exercising a benefit; and they don't even have to tell the People **what the benefit is**.

Some people think it's the driver's license, the marriage license, or the birth certificate, etc. I believe it's none of these.

SECTION 18: The Compelled Benefit.

I believe the **benefit being used** is that we have been given the privilege of **"discharging debt"** with limited liability, instead of **"paying debt"** with substance. When we pay a debt, we give substance for substance; equal value for equal value.

If I buy a quart of milk with a silver dollar, that dollar paid for the milk, and the milk paid for the dollar — substance for substance; pound for pound. But if I use a Federal Reserve to buy the milk, I have not paid for it. There is no substance in the Federal Reserve Note. It is **worthless paper** given in exchange for **something of substantive value.**

Congress offers us this **Remedy** in the form of a **benefit.** Debt money, fake money, authorized by the federal United States, can be spent all over the continental united States, it is declared legal tender for all debts, public and private, and the **limited liability** is that **you cannot be sued for not paying your debts** when you **"discharge"** the **"charge"** using this colorable money.

So they have said, "We're going to help you out; you can **"discharge"** your debts instead of **"paying"** your debts."

When we use this "colorable" money to discharge our debts, we cannot use Common Law courts. We can only use Colorable Law courts. We are under the jurisdiction of the UCC. We are using **non-redeemable negotiable instruments** and we are **discharging** debt rather than **paying** debts.

SECTION 19: Remedy And Recourse.

Every system of civilized law must have two characteristics, **Remedy and Recourse**. Remedy is a way to get out from under the law. Recourse is if you have been damaged under the law; you can recover your loss. The Common Law, the Law of Merchants, and even the UCC, all have **Remedy and Recourse**, but for a long time we could not find it. If you go to a law library and ask to see the UCC they will show you a shelf of books completely filled with the UCC. When you pick up one volume and start to read it, it will seem to have been intentionally written to be confusing. It took us a long time to discover where the

Remedy and Recourse are found in the UCC. They are found right in the first volume, at **UCC 1-207** and **1-103**.

SECTION 20: Remedy.

The making of a valid **Reservation of Rights** preserves whatever rights the person possessed at that time, and prevents the loss of such rights by application of the concepts of **waiver or estoppel**. (UCC 1-207.7)

It is important to remember when we go into a court that we are in a **commercial international jurisdiction**. If we go into court and say, "I DEMAND MY CONSTITUTIONAL RIGHTS," the judge will most likely say, "You mention the Constitution again and I'll find you **in contempt of court!**" We don't, then, understand how he can do that. Hasn't he sworn to uphold the Constitution? The rule here is this. You cannot be **"charged"** under one jurisdiction and **"defend"** under another. For example, if the French Government came to you and asked where you filed your French income tax for a certain year, do you go to the French Government and say, "I demand my Constitutional Rights?" No. The proper answer is "THE LAW DOESN'T APPLY TO ME — I'M NOT A FRENCHMAN." You must make your **reservation of rights** under the jurisdiction in which you are charged — not under some other jurisdiction. So in a UCC court you must claim your **reservation of rights** under the UCC 1-207. [**now changed to UCC 1-308**]

SECTION 21: UCC 1-308 Goes On To Say:

When a **waivable right or claim** is involved, the failure to make a **reservation thereof** causes a loss of the right, and bars it's assertion at a later date. (UCC 1-308.9)

You have to **make your claim known early**. Further it says: "The Sufficiency of the Reservation: Any expression indicating an intention to reserve rights, is sufficient, such as **"without**

prejudice". (UCC 1-308.4)

Whenever you sign any legal paper, that deals with the Federal Reserve Notes in any way — under your signature write: **"Without Prejudice"**, or **"Without Prejudice UCC 1-308"**. This reserves your rights. You can see, at 1-308.4 that you have sufficiently reserved your rights.

It is **very important** to understand just what this means. For example, one man who used this in regard to a traffic ticket was asked by the judge just what he meant by writing **"without prejudice"** on his statement to the court. He had not tried to understand the concepts involved. He only wanted to use it to get out of paying for the ticket. He did not know what it meant. When the judge asked him what he meant by signing in that way, he told the judge that he was not prejudice against anyone. The judge knew that the man had NO IDEA of what it meant so he lost the case. You must KNOW what it means.

SECTION 22: Without Prejudice UCC 1-308.

When you use **"without prejudice"** or **"without prejudice UCC 1-308"** in connection with your signature, you are saying: "I reserve my right not to be compelled to perform under any **contract** or **commercial agreement** that I did not enter KNOWINGLY, VOLUNTARILY, AND INTENTIONALLY — I do not accept the liability of any compelled benefit, or any unrevealed contract or commercial agreement.

What is the **compelled performance** of an unrevealed commercial agreement?

When you use Federal Reserve Notes instead of silver dollars, is it voluntary? No. There is no lawful money, so you **have to** use Federal Reserve Notes — you **have to** accept the benefit. The government has given you the benefit to discharge your debts. How nice they are! But if you **have not** reserved your rights under 1-308, you are **compelled** to accept the benefit, and are therefore **obligated** to obey every statue, ordinance, and regulation of the government, at all levels of government — federal, local, and state.

If you understand this, you will be able to explain it to the judge when he asks. And he **WILL** ask, so be prepared to explain this statement to the court. You will also need to understand **UCC 1-103 — Argument and Recourse**.

If you want to understand this fully, go to a law library and photocopy these two sections from the UCC. It is important to get the Anderson version. Some of the law libraries will only have the West Publishing version which is very difficult to understand. In Anderson, it is broken down with decimals into ten parts and most importantly, it is written in plain English.

SECTION 23: Recourse.

Recourse appears in **UCC at 1-103.6**, which says: "The Code is complimentary to the Common Law, which remains in force, except where displaced by the code. A statute should be construed in harmony with the Common Law, unless there is a clear legislative intent to abrogate the Common Law." (UCC 1-103.6)

This is the argument to use in court. The Code recognizes the Common Law. If it did not recognize the Common Law, the government would have to admit that **the United States is bankrupt and completely owned by its creditors**.

But it is not expedient to admit this. The Code was not written to entirely override the Common Law. Therefore, if you have made a sufficient, timely, and explicit **reservation of your rights** pursuant to **ICC 1-308**, you can insist that the statutes be construed in harmony with the Common Law.

If the charge is a traffic ticket, you may demand that the court **produce the injured person** who has filed a verified complaint. For example, if you were charged with failure to buckle your seat belt, you may ask the court who was injured as a result of your failure to "buckle up"?

However, if the judge won't listen to you, and just moves ahead with the case, you will want to read to him the last sentence of **UCC 1-103.6** which states that: The Code cannot be read to preclude a Common Law action.

Tell the Judge, "Your honor, I can sue you under the Common Law for violating my rights under the UCC." I have a Remedy, under the UCC to reserve my rights under the Common Law. I have exercised my Remedy, so you must construe this statue in harmony with the Common Law. To be in harmony with the Common Law, you must bring forth the damaged party.

[Note: Actually, it is better to use a rubber stamp, because this demonstrates that you had previously reserved your rights. The simple fact that it takes several days or a week to order and get a stamp shows that you had reserved your rights prior to signing the document. (Anderson Uniform Commercial Code Lawyers' Cooperative Publishing Co.)]

If the judge insists on proceeding with the case, act confused, and ask this question: "Let me see if I understand, Your Honor: Has this court made a legal determination that the Sections of 1-308 and 1-103 of the UCC, which is the system of law you are operating under, are not valid law before this court?

Now the judge is in a jamb. How can the court throw out one part of the Code and uphold another? If he answers, "yes", then you say: "I put this court on notice that I am appealing your legal determination."

Of course, the higher court will uphold the Code on appeal. The judge knows this, so you have boxed him into a corner.

SECTION 24: Practical Application In Traffic Court.

Just so we can understand how this whole process works, let's look at a court situation such as a traffic violation.

Assume you ran through a yellow light and a policeman gave you a traffic ticket.

1. The first thing you want to do is delay the action at least three weeks. This you can do by being pleasant and cooperative with the officer. Explain to him that you are very busy and ask if he could please set your court appearance for about three weeks away. (At this point we need to remember the government's trick: "I'm from the government, I'm here to help you." So we want to use this approach with them.)

2. The next step is to go to the clerk of the traffic court and say, "I believe it would be helpful if I talk to you, because I want to save the government some money (this will get his attention.) I am going to appeal this case. As you know, in an appeal, I have to have a transcript, but the traffic court doesn't have a court reporter. It would be a waste of taxpayers's money to run me through this court and then have to give me a trial 'de novo' (new trial) in a court of record. I need a transcript for appealing, and to save the government some money, maybe you could schedule me to appear in a court of record."

You can show the date on the ticket and the clerk will usually agree that there is plenty of time to schedule your trial for a court of record. Now, your first appearance is in a court of record and not in traffic court, where there is no record.

When you get into the court there will be a court reporter there who records every word the judge speaks, so that judge is much more careful in a court of record. You will be in a much better situation there than in traffic court. If there is no record, the judge can say whatever he wants — he can call you all sorts of names and tell you that you have no rights, and so on — and deny it later.

3. When you get into court, the judge will read the charges: driving through a yellow light, or whatever, and this is in violation of ordinance 'xyz'. He will then ask, "Do you understand the charge against you?"

4. "Well your Honor, there is a question I would like to ask before I can make a plea of innocent or guilty. I think it could be answered if I could put the officer on the stand for a moment and ask him a few short questions."

Judge: "I don't see why not. Let's swear in the officer and have him take the stand."

5. "Is this the instrument that you gave me?" (Handing him the traffic citation)

Officer: "Yes, this is a copy of it; the judge has the other part of it."

"Where did you get my address that you wrote on the citation?"

Officer: "Well I got it from your driver's license."

[Number 4 above is very important to get into the record, clearly stating that you do not understand the charges. With that in the record, the court cannot move forward to judge the facts. This will be covered later on.]

(Handing the officer you driver's license) "Is this the document you copied my name and address from?"

Officer: "Yes, this is where I got it."

"While you've got that in your hand, would you read the signature that's on that license?" (The officer reads the signature) "While you're there, would you read into the record what it says under the signature?"

Officer: "It says, Without Prejudice UCC 1-308."

Judge: "Let me see that license!" (He looks and turns to the officer) "You didn't notice this printing under the signature on this license when you copied his name and address onto the ticket?"

Officer: "Oh no. I was just getting the address — I didn't look down there."

Judge: "You're not very observant as an officer. Therefore, I'm afraid I cannot accept your testimony in regards to the facts of this case. This case is dismissed."

6. In this case, the Judge found a convenient way out — he could say that the officer was not observant enough to be a reliable witness. He did not want to admit the **real nature of the jurisdiction** of his court. Once it was in the record that you had written "Without Prejudice UCC 1-308" on your license, the judge knew that he would have to admit:

    a. ...that you had reserved your Common Law rights under the UCC;

    b. ...that you had done it sufficiently by writing "Without prejudice UCC 1-308" on your driver's license;

    c. ...that the statute would now have to be read in harmony with the Common Law, and the Common Law says that the statute exists, but there is no injured party;

    d. ...that since there is no injured party or complaining witness, the court has no jurisdiction under the Common Law.

7. If the judge tries to move ahead anyway and try the facts of the case, you will want to ask him the following question: "Your Honor, let me understand this correctly: has this court made a legal determination that it has authority under the jurisdiction that it is operating under, to ignore two sections of the Uniform Commercial Code which have been called to it's attention?"

If he says yes, tell him that you put the court on notice that you will appeal his legal determination, and that if you are damaged by his actions, you will sue him in a common law action under the jurisdiction of the UCC. This will work just as well with the Internal Revenue Service. In fact, we can use the UCC with the IRS before we even get to court.

SECTION 25: Using The Code With The IRS.

If the IRS sends you a **Notice of Deficiency** this is called a **"presentment"** in the UCC. A "presentment" in the UCC is very similar to the Common Law. First we must understand just how this works in the Common Law.

Suppose I get a man's name from a phone book — someone I have never meet. And I send him a bill, or invoice, on a nice letterhead, which says, **"For services rendered $10,000.00"** and I send this to him by **certified mail, return receipt requested** at the address taken from the phone book. The man has to sign for it before he can open it, so I get a **green card receipt** that he received it. When he opens it, he finds an invoice for $10,000 and the following statement: "If you have any questions concerning this bill or the services rendered, you have thirty days to make your questions or objections known."

Of course he has never heard of me, so he just throws the bill away and assumes that I'm confused or crazy. At the end of thirty days, I go to court and get a default judgment against him. He received a bill for $10,000 and was given thirty days to respond. He **failed to object to it, or ask any questions about it**. Now he has **defaulted on the bill** and I can **lawfully collect** the $10,000. This is common law.

The UCC works on the same principle. The minute you get a **Notice of Deficiency** from the IRS, return it immediately with a letter that says:

"The presentment above is dishonored. (Your name) has

reserved all of his rights under the Uniform Commercial Code at UCC 1-308.

This should be all that is necessary, as there is nothing more that they can do. In fact, I recently helped someone in Maine who received a **Notice of Deficiency**.

The man sent a letter such as this, dishonoring the "presentment." The IRS wrote back saying that they could not make a determination at that office, but were turning it over to the Collections Department. A letter was attached from the Collections Department, which said that they were sorry for the inconvenience they had caused him, and that the **NOD** had been withdrawn. So you can see that if it's handled properly these things are easily resolved.

SECTION 26: Impending Bankruptcy.

On my way here, I had a chance to visit with the Governor of _____. He is very concerned that if he runs for office this November, that there won't be a State at the end of four years. He believes that **the International Bankers might foreclose on the nation and officially admit that they own the whole world**.

They could round up everybody in the state capital building, put them in an internment camp and hold them indefinitely. They may give them a trial, or they may not. They may do whatever they want. As I explained earlier, it has not been expedient to foreclose on the nation until they could get everything ready. This is where the **Federal Emergency Management Agency** comes in. It has been put in place without anyone really noticing it.

SECTION 27: FEMA.

FEMA or the **Federal Emergency Management Agency** has been designed for **when America is officially declared bankrupt**, which would be a **national emergency**. In a national emergency, **all Constitutional Rights and all law that previously existed would be suspended**. FEMA has created large concentration camps where they would put anyone who might cause trouble **for the orderly plan and process of the new regime** to take over the nation.

Even a Governor could be thrown into one of these internment camps and kept there indefinitely. This is all in place now and they are just waiting to declare a national emergency.

Then even the state governments could be dissolved. Anybody who might oppose **the new regime** could be imprisoned until **a new set of laws** could be written and **a new government set up**. The Governor knows all this and he is very concerned. He doesn't want to be in office when all this happens.

I [Harold Freeman] visited with him and I told him that there are certain actions we should take right now. I think that we should consider the fact that, according to the UCC, each State is an **accommodation party to the national debt**. To understand this we must realize that **there are two separate entities** known as the **"United States"**.

<u>SECTION 28:</u> The Rothschild Influence.

When America was founded, the Rothschilds were very unhappy because it was founded on the **Christian Common Law**. The **Common Law** is based on **substance** and this substance is mentioned in the Constitution as **silver and gold**.

America is a **Constitutional Republic** which is a Union of the States **under the Constitution**.

When Congress was working for the Republic **the only thing Congress could borrow or issue was silver or gold**, and the Rothschild Banks did not lend silver or gold. Naturally, they did not like this new government.

The Rothschilds had a deal with the King of England. The King would **borrow paper** and agree to **repay in gold**. But these United States, **with their Constitution,** were an obstacle to the Rothschilds, and it was much to the their advantage to get the colonies back under the King. So the Rothschilds financed **the War of 1812** to bring America back under the British Crown. It didn't work as planned so they had to find another way.

SECTION 29: The Flaw In The Constitution, Two Nations In One.

Around the time of the American Civil War, they discovered a flaw in the Constitution. The flaw was Art. I, Sect. 3, Clause 17.

Remember, **there are <u>two nations</u> called the "United States."**

What is a nation? See if you agree with this definition:

Whenever there is a **governing body** having a **prescribed territory containing a body of people**. [This is an easy to understand restatement of the definition presented in Black's Law Dictionary]

Is this a nation? Yes. We have a **governing body** in the Republic; **a three-branch government**; legislative, executive, and judicial branches, under a Constitution. We have a **prescribed territory containing a body of people**, as a **Constitutional Republic**.

But, **Article I, Sect. 8, Clause 17** gave Congress (**the legislative branch of the three branch government**) exclusive rule over a different territory containing a body of people (**District of Columbia**). Here we have **a nation within a nation** — a **Legislative Democracy** within a **Constitutional Republic**.

When Congress was part of a Constitutional Republic, it was obligated to provide a medium of exchange for the People.

Its duty was to coin silver and gold. Anyone who had a piece of silver or gold could bring it in and have it freely minted into silver or gold coin. This was the medium of exchange for the Republic.

But **in the Legislative Democracy** (over Washington DC) **Congress is not limited by the Constitution**. Congress has exclusive rule over the **District of Columbia and its People**.

The legislators in the **District of Columbia** can make the laws by a majority vote, because the **District of Columbia** is a Democracy wherein their administrative agents enforce their own laws; and the administrative courts in their government try their own laws. Here we have the legislature **making the law, enforcing the law, and trying the law**, all **within the one branch** of government. This is **a one branch government; within a three branch government**.

Under the **three-branch government**, Congress passes laws which must be in harmony with the Constitution, the executive enforces these laws passed by Congress, and the judiciary tries these laws passed by Congress, pursuant to the Constitution.

THE THREE-BRANCH CONSTITUTIONAL REPUBLIC AND THE ONE-BRANCH LEGISLATIVE DEMOCRACY **Both called the "United States"**. One is the **continental United States**. The other is the **federal United States (Federal Zone)**.

SECTION 30: Are You A United States Citizen?

If you say that you are a **United States citizen**, which United States are you referring to?

Anyone who lives in the **District of the Columbia** is a **citizen of the United States**. The remaining population in the union of fifty states are **National Citizens** of the nation. We are **domiciled** in the various sovereign states; and **protected** by the constitutions of those states from any **direct rule of Congress over us**.

In the democracy, anyone who lives in the states known as **Washington DC, Guam, Puerto Rico,** or any of the other **federally held territories** is a <u>**citizen of the United States**</u> **(D.C.)**

We must be careful with our choice of words — **we are not** <u>**citizens of the United States**</u>. We are not **subject to Congress**. Congress has exclusive rule over a **given territory** and **we are not part of that territory**.

Where did Congress get the authority to write the **Internal Revenue Code**? It is found in **Art. I, Sect. 8 Clause 17** of the Constitution. To pass that law **they only needed a majority vote**. There is no other way that they can pass laws directly affecting individuals. **Title 26** (the Internal Revenue Code), was passed as law for **a different nation**. (Remember our definition of "nation"). **Title 26 is not consistent with the Bill of Rights**. If you try to fight the IRS, you have no rights — the IRS Code does not give you your Constitutional rights. It simply says, "you failed to file an income tax form — you failed to perform in some specific manner."

Remember, under the **Common Law**, you are free to do whatever you want to do as long as you do not infringe upon the life, liberty, or property of anybody else. If you do not want to perform, you don't have to. The only way you can be compelled to perform **under the Constitution** of the **continental united States** is if you have voluntarily entered into a contract. But if you are not under a contract **you cannot be compelled to perform**. You cannot be compelled to file an income tax form.

When Congress **works for the Republic**, every law it passes must be in harmony with the Constitution and the Bill of Rights, but when Congress **works for the Legislative Democracy**, any law it passes becomes the law only **over federal territory**.)

If you are charged with **Willful Failure to File** a 1040 income tax form, that form is of and for a different nation. You're a **non-resident alien** of that **nation**. It is a foreign corporation to you. It is not the **Republic of the continental United States** coming after you; **it is a foreign nation** — the **legislative democracy of a foreign nation** coming after you.

If you get a **Notice of Deficiency** from the IRS, it is a **presentment from the federal United States**, so you can **use the UCC to dishonor it**, and you can tell the IRS that you are among the **National Citizenry of the continental united States**; that you are a **non-resident alien** to the **federal United States**.

You never lived in the **Federal Zone** (a federal territory) and you never had any income from the **federal United States**.

Furthermore, you cannot be required to **file or pay taxes** under the **compelled benefit** of using the Federal Reserve Notes, because you have **reserved your rights** under the **Common Law** through **UCC 1-308**.

SECTION 31: Original Intent of the Founders.

The Founding Fathers would never have created a government that was going to boss them around! There were 13 sovereign States. They were Nations which they joined **together in Union** for protection from foreign enemies. They provided a means by which the **union of sovereign states** could fend off foreign and domestic enemies. But they never gave **the Congress of the federal United States** direct rule over **any citizen of any union state**. They were not going to be ordered around by the government that they set up.

SECTION 32: Federal Region — the Federal Zone.

The Supreme Court has declared that **Congress can rule what Congress creates**. Congress did **NOT** create the **States**; but Congress **DID** create **federal regions**. So Congress can rule the **federal regions**, but Congress **CANNOT** rule the States.

How have we been tricked into Federal regions?

SECTION 33: The Zip Code Trick.

Remember how the government always comes to use and says, "I'm from the government, and I've come to help you out." The government went to the various states and said, "We don't want you to go to all that trouble of writing three or four letters to abbreviate the name of your state — such as **Ariz.** for Arizona, just write **AZ** instead of **Ariz.** Or you can just write **WY** for **Wyoming** instead of **Wyo.**" So all of the states of the union have been given **new two-letter abbreviations**. Even a state such as **Rhode Island** has a new abbreviation; **RI** instead of **R.I.** They just left off the periods. When you use a **two-letter state abbreviation**, you are compelled to use the **zip code** (the **Z**one **Im**provement **C**ode) because there are many states which start with the same letter. For example, **"M"**. **ME** is Maine - **MI** is Michigan - **MS** is Mississippi. With **MA, MO, MN, MS,** etc and some sloppy writing, and you could not tell one from another. So we use the **zip code** in order to tell them apart. But if you wrote **Mich.** or **Minn.**, or **Miss.**, there would be no problem telling them apart.

There's no harm in using the **zip code**, if you lawfully identify your state. I found out that no state legislature has met to lawfully change the abbreviation of their state from it's old abbreviation to the new. Therefore, if you do not use the **lawful abbreviation** for your state, but use the new **legal shorter abbreviation**, you have to use the **zip code**.

Look on page 11 of the **Zip Code Directory**, and it will tell you that the **first digit** of your zip code is the **federal region** in which you **reside**. If you use **AZ** for **Arizona**, you cannot use the state constitution to protect you because you did not lawfully identify your state. You used the **zip code**, which identifies which **federal region** you live in. Congress may rule federal regions directly, but it cannot rule the **citizens of any state**.

SECTION 34: Accommodation Party.

Let's look at how the states have become the **accommodation party** to the national debt. Many people who I have talked to — including the Governor — are very concerned about this and know that it could happen very soon.

If America is declared a **bankrupt nation**, it will be a **national emergency**. FEMA will take over and anyone who opposes the Creditors new government can be sent to a detention camp in Alaska. We will have no rights whatsoever.

They have already setup prison camps with work camps nearby so the people can be used for slave labor. It could be the governors, legislators and other leaders who would be hauled away to Alaska, while the people now disenfranchised from power would likely be chosen to run the new government. This could all happen very soon, as the national debt is so large as to be unpayable. Even the interest on the debt is virtually unpayable.

As I explained, **the national debt** — more than three trillion dollars — [now $17 trillion dollars] **is not owed by the Continental United States**. It is owed by the **federal United States** that was given the authority to borrow bank credit. When Congress worked for the Continental united States, it could only borrow silver and gold, therefore the **national debt was borrowed by the federal United States**.

The federal United States had to **trap the States** into assuming the **debt obligation** of the federal debt.

In the UCC, we find the term, **"accommodation party"**. How did the states become the **"accommodation party"** to the federal debt? The federal government forced the states **to deal in Federal Reserve Notes**, which means that everything that the states do and have done is "colorable". Under the "colorable" jurisdiction of the UCC all of the states are **accommodation parties** to the federal debt.

The concern now is to find out how we can get out of this situation. I told the Governor that in the **Common Law** and the **Law of Merchants** (the International Law Merchant) there's a term called **"no-interest contract"**. A **"no-interest contract"** is unenforceable and void. What is a **"no-interest contract"**?

SECTION 35: No-Interest Contract.

If I were to insure a house that did not belong to me, that would be a **no-interest contract**. I would just want the house to burn down. I would pay a small premium, perhaps a few hundred dollars, and insure it for $80,000 against fire. Then I would be waiting for the house to burn down so I could trade my small premium for $80,000. I would have **"no interest"** in living in or owning the house.

Under the Common Law, this is called a **"no-interest" contract**, which is unenforceable in any court and therefore void.

SECTION 36: Unconscionable Contracts.

No-interest contracts are called **Unconscionable contracts**. The section in the **Anderson Code** on Unconscionable contracts covers more than forty pages! The **federal United States** has made each state an **accommodation party** to the federal debt, which could be proven to be **an Unconscionable contract**.

We should get some **litigation into the courts** (before the government declares a national emergency) claiming that this state has **no lawful responsibility for the national debt** (of the federal United States) because it became an accommodation party to this debt through an **Unconscionable, No-interest contract**.

If we have this litigation before the courts under **International Law** when the nation is declared bankrupt, the Creditors would have to settle this matter first, and it would delay them. They would want the **new government** to appear legitimate, so they could not just move right in and take over the state, because it would be in an **International Court**. This is very important at this time.

SECTION 37: Questions and Review.

Note: These are some of the questions asked after the main lecture. Some are restatements of material presented earlier, but they contain valuable information worth repeating.

SECTION 38: Courtroom Techniques.

Q. How did you "box in" the Judge?

A. This is easy to do if you don't know too much. I didn't know too much, but I boxed them in. You must play a little dumb. If you are arrested and you go into court, just remember that in a criminal action, **you must understand the law,** or it is a reversible error for the court to try you. **If you don't understand the law, they can't try you** and have to dismiss the case.

In any traffic case, or tax case, you are called into court and the judge reads the law and then asks, Do you understand the charges?

Defendant: No, Your Honor, I do not.

Judge: Well, what is so difficult about that charge? Either you drove the wrong way on a one-way street or you did not. You can only go one way on that street, and if you go the other way it's a fifty-dollar fine. What's so difficult about this that you do not understand?

Defendant: Well, Your Honor, it's not the **letter** of the law, but rather the **nature** of the law that I don't understand. The Sixth Amendment to the Constitution gives me the right to ask the court to explain the **nature and cause** of any action against me, and upon my request the court has the **duty to answer**. I have a question about the **nature and cause** of this action.

Judge: Well, what is that; what do you want to know?

Defendant: Well Your Honor, is this a **civil or criminal action**?

Judge: It is criminal. (If it were a civil action, there could be no fine so it has to be criminal.)

Defendant: Thank you, Your Honor, for telling me that. Then the record will show that this action against (your name) is a criminal action, is that right?

Judge: Yes.

Defendant: I would like to ask another question about this criminal action. There are **two criminal jurisdictions** mentioned in the Constitution: one is under the **Common Law**, and the other deals with **International Maritime Contracts** under Admiralty Jurisdiction.

Equity is Civil, and you said this is a **Criminal action**, so it seems it would have to be under either **Common Law** or **Maritime Law**. But what puzzles me, Your Honor, is that there is no *corpus delicti* here to give this court **jurisdiction** over **my person and property** under the Common Law. Therefore, it doesn't appear that this court is moving under **Common Law**.

Judge: No. This court is not under the **Common Law**.

Defendant: Well, thank you, Your Honor, but now you make the charge against me even more difficult to understand. The only other **criminal jurisdiction** would apply only 1.) if there was an **International Maritime Contract** involved, 2.) I was a party to it, 3.) it had been breached, and 4.) the court was operating in an **Admiralty Jurisdiction**.

I don't believe I have ever been under any **International Maritime contract**, so I would deny that one exists. I would have to demand **that such a contract**, if one does exist, **be placed**

into evidence, so that I may contest it. But surely this court is not operating in an **Admiralty Jurisdiction**.

You just put the words in the judge's mouth.

Judge: No, I can assure you, we're not operating in an Admiralty Jurisdiction. We're not out in the ocean somewhere, — we're right here in the middle of the state. No this is not an Admiralty Jurisdiction.

Defendant: Thank you Your Honor, but now I am more puzzled than ever. If this charge is not under the Common Law nor under Admiralty and those are the only two criminal jurisdictions mentioned in the Constitution — what kind of jurisdiction could this court be operating under?

Judge: It's Statutory Jurisdiction.

Defendant: Oh, thank you, Your Honor. I'm glad you told me that. But I have never heard of that jurisdiction. So if I have to defend myself under that jurisdiction, I would need to have the **Rules of Criminal Procedure for Statutory Jurisdiction**. Can you tell me where I might find such rules?

(There are no rules for Statutory Jurisdiction so the judge will get very angry at this point and say):

Judge: If you want answers to questions like that, get a licensed attorney — I'm not allowed to practice law from the bench.

Defendant: Oh, Your Honor, I don't think anyone would accuse you of **practicing law from the bench** if you just answered a few questions to explain to me the **nature and cause of this action** so that I can defend myself.

Judge: I told you before, I am not going to answer any more questions. Do you understand that? If you ask anymore questions in regards to this, I'm going to find you **in contempt of**

court! Now if you can't afford a licensed attorney, the court will appoint one for you. But if you want those questions answered, you must get a licensed attorney.

Defendant: Thank you, Your Honor, but let me just see if I got this straight. Has this court made a legal determination that it has authority to conduct a criminal action against me, the accused, **under a secret jurisdiction**, the rules of which are known only to this court and licensed attorneys, thereby denying me that right to defend myself in my own person?

He has no answer for that. The judge will probably postpone the case and eventually just let it go. In this way, you can be wise as a serpent and as harmless as a dove, but you must not go into court with a chip on your shoulder and as a wolf in "black sheep" country. Remember Jesus' words, *"I send you forth as sheep in the midst of wolves, be ye therefore wise as serpents, and harmless as doves."* Sheep do not attack wolves directly. Just be an innocent lamb who just can't understand the charge, and remember — they can't try you criminally if you don't understand the charge. That would automatically be a reversible error on appeal.

<u>**SECTION 39:**</u> The Social Security Problem.

If I were a young man, 18 or 20 years old and just starting out in my first job, I would not want Social Security. Along with my signature on the application I would write **"Without Prejudice UCC 1-308"** to reserve my Common Law rights. But why wouldn't I want Social Security today?

I got into the Social Security system in the 1930's and I paid into it dollars that had good purchasing power. Now I'm getting a promised return in Federal Reserve Notes which have considerably less value. For example, in 1940 you could buy a deluxe Chevrolet automobile for $800 dollars. With today's Federal Reserve Notes that won't buy the rear fenders and trunk on a new Chevrolet. If I were a young man, I would not want to put Federal Reserve Notes into SS now, and get back something later, like the German Mark after WWI when it took a billion Marks to buy a loaf of bread.

They will give you every Federal Reserve Note back they promised you but it might not buy anything.

SECTION 40: Assurance of Performance.

Under The UCC You have the right in any agreement to **demand a guarantee of performance**. So, don't go to them and say, "I want to rescind my SSN" — or "I refuse to take it." Just go easy and say, **"I would be happy to get a Social Security Number** and enter into this contract, but I have a little problem. How can I have **assurance** before I enter into this contract that the purchasing power of the Federal Reserve Notes I get back at the end of the contract will be as good as the ones that I pay in at the beginning.

They can't guarantee that, and you have a right (under the UCC) to **assurance of performance** of the contract.

So tell them, "Well, I cannot enter this contract unless the government will guarantee to pay me at the end of the contract with the same value Federal Reserve Notes that I'm paying in. Both may be called Federal Reserve Notes, but you know that these Federal Reserve Notes don't hold their value. I want **assurance** on this contract that the Federal Reserve Notes that I get in my retirement will buy as much as the ones I'm giving you now in my working years." They can't make that guarantee. If they won't give you that guarantee, just say, "I'd be glad to sign this but if you can't **guarantee performance under the contract**, I'm afraid I can not enter the contract."

Now did **YOU** refuse or did **THEY** refuse? You can get the sections of the UCC which grant the **right to assurance** that the contract you have entered will be properly fulfilled — that the return will equal the investment — or you can **reject the contract using the Code**. Using their own system of law, you can show that they cannot make you get into a contract of that nature. Just approach them innocently like a lamb.

It is very important to be gentle and humble in all dealings with the government or the courts — never raise your voice or show anger. In the courtroom, always be polite, and build the judge up — call him "Your Honor." Give him all the "honor" that he actually deserves. He didn't rise to his position by standing on his thumbs. It does no good to be difficult, but rather be cooperative and ask questions in a way that leads the judge to say the things which you need to have in the record.

SECTION 41: The Court Reporter

In many courts, there will be a regular court reporter. He gets his job at the judge's pleasure, so he doesn't want to displease the judge. The court reporter is sworn to give an accurate transcript of every word that is spoken in the courtroom. But if the judge makes a slip of the tongue, he might turn to **HIS** court reporter and say, "I think you had better leave that out of the transcript; just say it got a little to far ahead of you, and you couldn't quite get everything in." So this will be missing from the transcript. In one case, we brought a licensed court reporter with us and the judge got very angry and said, "This court has a licensed court reporter right here, and the record of this court is this court reporter's record. No other court reporter's record means anything in this court."

We responded with, "Of course, Your Honor, we're certainly glad to use your regular court reporter. But you know, Your Honor, sometimes things move so fast that a court reporter gets a little behind, and doesn't quite keep up with it all. Wouldn't it be nice if we had **another licensed court reporter in the courtroom,** just in case your court reporter got a little behind, so that we could fill in from this **other court reporter's data**? I'm sure, Your Honor, that you want an accurate transcript. (I like to use the saying; **give a bad dog a good name, and he'll live up to it!**)

The judge went along with it, and from that moment on, he was very careful of what he said. These are little tricks to getting around in court. This is how to be wise as a serpent and harmless as a dove when we enter a courtroom. There are others using the same information presented here who end up in jail, hand-cuffed and hit over the head, **because they approached the situation with a chip on their shoulder**. They try to tell the judge what the law is and that he is a no-good scoundrel and so on. Just be harmless and wise.

SECTION 42: UCC 1-308 Review

It is so important to know and understand the meaning of **"without prejudice UCC 1-308"** in connection with your signature, that we go over this once more. It is very likely that a judge will ask you what this means. So please learn and understand this carefully:

> "The use of **Without prejudice UCC 1-308** in connection with my signature indicates that I have reserved my Common Law right NOT TO BE COMPELLED TO PERFORM under any contract I did not enter into KNOWINGLY, VOLUNTARILY, and INTENTION-ALLY. And, I do not accept the liability associated with the compelled benefit of any UN-REVEALED CONTRACT OR COMMERCIAL AGREEMENT."

Once you state this, this is all the judge needs to hear. Under Common Law, **both parties must enter into a contract knowingly, voluntarily, and intentionally, or it can be declared unenforceable and void.**

You are claiming the right not to be compelled to perform under any contract that you did not enter into knowingly, voluntarily and intentionally. And you do not accept the liability associated with the compelled benefit of any unrevealed contract or agreement.

The compelled benefit is the **privilege** to use Federal Reserve Notes to discharge your debts with limited liability rather than to pay your debts with silver or gold coins. It is a **compelled benefit** because there are no silver or gold coins in circulation.

You have to eat and you can only buy food with a medium of exchange provided by the government. You are not allowed to print your own money so you are **compelled to use theirs**. This is the **compelled benefit of an undisclosed commercial agreement**.

If you have not made a valid, timely and explicit reservation of your rights under UCC 1-308 and you exercise this benefit of **using paper non-federal Federal Reserve Notes offered by the government**, you will be obligated under an **implied agreement** to obey every statute, ordinance and regulation passed by government at all levels — federal, local, and state.

SECTION 43: CONCLUSION

The editor of this transcript has taken great liberties in putting this to paper in an effort to make it readable and somewhat compact. He wishes to offer his gratitude to Howard Freeman for the opportunity to work with the information so absolutely vital to our survival as dignified, unenslaved human beings. He must also ask Mr. Freeman's forgiveness for any errors committed in getting this to print. Its purpose, as stated in the Foreword, is to make this knowledge and wisdom available to as many people as will take the time to read it. This is meant to be supplemental to Mr. Freeman's recorded lectures, not a substitute.

Indeed, there is **NO SUBSTITUTE** for hearing him present this material in his own words. It is not just the **LAW** and the **FACTS** that are important here, but the **WAY** they are used. His numerous reminders of Jesus' commission **to be "like sheep among wolves"** cannot be overstated, and is certainly good advice to us — in all dealings — not just in court or with the government. Hearing him explain this in his own words brings to life the practical application and usefulness of being "harmless and wise". In fact, after being introduced to this approach, it becomes difficult to imagine that any other way of defending oneself from the government would be effective.

Having said that, I feel obliged to point out that one of the most difficult aspects of dealing with a licensed attorney — even a good one — may be knowing whose side he is on. (**After all, HE IS AN OFFICER OF THE COURT.**)

So for those of use who have concluded that having an attorney means that you will soon be chained, gagged and led to the gallows, this information may be in-dispensable. For the extraordinary challenges of appearing in court in one's own person — *"pro per"* — there are few reliable sources of information. Learning to defend ourselves, that is, being **"responsible"** instead of turning **one more area** of our lives over to **"professionals"** — may be the only way to have any chance of digging ourselves out of legal tyranny.

Perhaps the greatest problem we face in education today is the matter of **widespread legal illiteracy**. Naturally, there will always be a number of people who just don't care about these issues who either:

1.) ...have a soft life supported and maintained by this secret system of institutions and law which has grown up around us.

(*"I can make a bundle buying these IRS seized homes cheap and reselling them"*);

2.) ...don't believe that anything can be done about it. (*"You can't fight city hall"*);

3.) ...don't have the energy or inclination to do anything about it. (*"That's nice, but let's see what's on TV"*).

For those good "citizens" this whole effort may seem useless or even threatening. But it is this writers view that God did not intend for us to spend our lives in statutory slavery for the benefit of a handful of secret world manipulators, even if the "masters" grant us some token of diversions and pleasure.

Human dignity requires much more than entertainment. The door is there and the key exists; we must find it and we must use it to return to freedom!

Let us discover the mistakes we have made, let us find the truth, let us apply it with meekness and wisdom, and let us gently but firmly reclaim the precious liberty and freedom which we have so foolishly given up.

Well there you have it, The UCC Connection. There is also a list of other publications available from the Common Law Grand Jury website **NationalLibertyAlliance.org**

If you found this information useful, I recommend contacting us for a list of our materials. We hope we didn't put in all this effort only for someone to say, "Yea, that's on the Internet..."

We tried to find stuff like this for some time now and other than John Freeman's articles, we found none. Also, we like the author's approach here. Many of the so-called "patriot" organizations seem to be more "profiteers" than patriots. We understand that bills need to be paid, but after reading lists and lists of **"products available for $xxxx"** we see this pamphlet as a little different.

Good luck, and God bless...

THE UCC CONNECTION

"I send you forth as sheep in the midst of wolves, be ye therefore wise as serpents, and harmless as doves."

And a few more quotes:

"When even one American (who has done nothing wrong) is forced by fear to shut his mind and close his mouth, then all Americans are in peril." (former President Harry Truman).

"In the beginning of a change, the patriot is a scarce man, brave hated and scorned. When his cause succeeds however, the timid join him, for then it costs nothing to be a patriot." (Mark Twain).

"Truth is less than truth until it is made known." (John Wheeler).

In memory of Harold Freeman who left us in 1992.

SPECIAL STUFF YOU SHOULD KNOW

Taking Your Birth Certificate to Court

The courts only want to **charge** some bogus bonds to your **federal account**, and they need your **bond** or **permission** to do the discharge. **Otherwise you must pay a fine and go to jail.** But they neglected to tell us that **the birth certificate is the bond.** And the birth certificate is **proof that we are the beneficiary** and not the trustee of **our strawman trust account**. The state is the **trustee.**

Everything including crime and taxes **is already pre-paid** through that **birth certificate bond.**

In every case so far, **the charges were settled** and they let the fellow go without a record of crime **by surrendering the birth certificate.**

Further, the **birth certificate** proves that **you are the beneficiary** of your strawman estate.

The **prosecutor** is claiming that he represents **the beneficiary** (the state) when **the state is really suppose to be the trustee.**

So when you bring the **birth certificate** into court, **you discharge all of the charges against you**. And you prove that **you are the beneficiary of your trust estate**. And this completely shuts the prosecutor down.

The **prosecutor** now **has no standing.** You bringing in the **birth certificate** proves that **he has brought fraud into the cour**t by claiming to be the **beneficiary** instead of you.

Only the **beneficiary (YOU)** can be the **plaintiff.** And only the **trustee (the state)** can be the **defendant**.

I do not give legal advice, **but this is what I would do** if I were in your shoes.

HOW TO PROCEED

1.   **Take a certified copy of your birth certificate** (*certified by the state*) **to court with you.** DO NOT MAKE A

COPY - OR IT IS VOID! DO NOT MARK ON IT - OR IT IS VOID!

2.   **Write down what you are going to say,** you will be nervous and forgetful.

3.   When they call your name, **walk up to the bar** but do not cross it. If it is a court of record, **ask them "Are we on the record?"** Once you are satisfied you're on the record you can proceed. If they ask your name, ask again, **"Are we on the record"?**

(If it's a misdemeanor, a lot of times there is no record, so just proceed.)

4.   Hand the Birth certificate across the bar and say, **"I am here on 'special appearance'. Let the record show that the 'person' and 'birth certificate' has been surrendered to the court."**

If they will not come and take the Birth Certificate, **then gently toss it across the bar** into the well of the court.

(**NOTE:** A **'person'** is a **legal fiction. You are a living soul**. A living soul is **not** a **'person'**.) ("Special apprerance" means that **you are not giving the court jurisdiction over you**.)

5.   Then turn around and leave. **Do not stop, do not answer questions**.

When they say "Hey you, stop", or "You have a court date on such and such..." **...just keep on going, and get out. DO NOT RESPOND!!! DO NOT COME BACK!!!**

Do not let them bluff you into coming back. At the time of this writing, this approach has worked 100% of the time. However, about 5% of the folks who do this, report that **the court tries to threaten them with letters**.

The worse that may happen is that **they send you a bill** for whatever you're accused of, and possibly the **threat of an arrest warrant**.

Sometimes they'll send a letter **with a new court date**. And the very latest was a **threat letter** saying **that there was an arrest warrant**. Or threatening you with arrest **if you do not**

come in to be arraigned.

However, if they could have issued or served a warrant, they would have. So this has all been **a bluff 100% of the time**.

Even in the letter that said there was an arrest warrant (there *was* one on record) but **it was never processed or served**.

Bluff, bluff , bluff. If you receive any of these letters, **mail them back** with a regular letter stating that **"I reserve all of my rights per UCC 1-308 and I do not consent"**.

Do not enter anything into the record or place a court heading at the top of your letter — **or that will be giving consent**.

A regular letter only. Only once has anyone reported being grabbed while leaving the court. And this man was still successful in leaving without prosecution.

ALTERNATE METHOD

Simply telling the court that **"I reserve all of my rights per UCC 1-308"** and they would immediately let you go, **before. But not anymore**. They keep coming against you trying to trick you into their jurisdiction. Which most People fall for.

Filing documents into their court, and motions, **gives them jurisdiction**, so they take the opportunity to **deny everything** and keep on working against you.

However, **UCC 1-308 is the remedy to the courts**, so it is a matter of figuring out **how to apply it** without **giving jurisdiction**.

The following method is almost the same as the birth certificate method above.

THE ALTERNATIVE PROCESS

1. **Take a certified copy of your birth certificate** (*certified by the state*) **to court with you.** DO NOT MAKE A COPY - OR IT IS VOID! DO NOT MARK ON IT - OR IT IS VOID!

2. **Write down what you are going to say,** you will be nervous and forgetful.

3. When they call your name, **you walk up to the bar** but do not cross it. If it is a court of record, **ask them "Are we on**

the record?" Once you are satisfied that you're on the record you can proceed. If they ask your name, ask again, **"Are we on the record"?**

(If it is a misdemeanor, a lot of times there is no record, so just proceed.)

4. Then say, "**I am here on special appearance. Let the record show that I,** (your *first name* only) **reserve all of my rights per UCC 1-308 and I do not consent**."

5. Then turn around and leave. **Do not stop, do not answer any questions**. When they say "Hey you, stop" ...**keep on going and get out**.

The following is a **suggested way** to handle the situation for **the one fellow that might get grabbed**.

Do not resist if they lay hands on you, and force you into the well of the court. If they do **do not answer to any name**. If they say "Mr. Whatever your name is" while talking to you, say "**I am not that person**, I am **the beneficiary** and **I reserve all of my rights per UCC 1-308**".

The judge may start asking you questions like who are you, your name and address, and etc.. **This is all a trick to get you into his jurisdiction**. Once you give them your full name or address, **they have you**. Simply say, "**That is immaterial, I am the beneficiary** and **I reserve all of my rights per UCC 1-308.**"

If they ask what to call you, simply say "**You can call me the beneficiary**".

If the judge threatens you with contempt for not giving your name or answering his questions, simply ask, "**Can anything I say be used against me?**" They usually will not answer you or they may say "**Yes**". **Then you remain silent**.

If he threatens you over and over, keep asking, "**Can anything I say be used against me?**" Or you can answer, "**I do not understand**". Sometimes they will take **your ID** from your wallet and ask you why your picture is on it. Say, "**That proves I am the beneficiary**"

(**NOTE:** You had to show your **birth certificate** to get a social security number or drivers license because, **the birth certificate proves you are the beneficiary** who can receive it.)

If the judge tries to find you in contempt for not answering, **others reported** only **being held for a few hours** as a scare tactic; **then they were let go**. They cannot do anything to you unless you give them your name and/or address.

Ever noticed that a cop asks, or yells "**What is your name?!!**" (**They have to have your name to do anything to you**.)

Then ask "**Is the matter is settled?**" They will try to hand the birth certificate back to you, but **do not take it unless and until** they say **the matter is settled, excused** or something to that effect.

If the judge leaves the court room, **he is trying to restart the proceedings because you have won**. So say, "**Let the record show that the judge has abandoned the case, and now the case is closed with prejudice.**" And then leave.

The only thing you may get is **a nasty threat** of a **bench warrant in the mail** or an **order to pay a fine**. But this would be **onlya trick**. If they could do anything at all, there would be an **arrest warrant** the first day.

I would **make notes** before I go in. So you do not loose track of what you are doing. Once you get nervous **its hard to remember everything**.

I always **take my time** and do not let them rush me. **Talk slowly**. They only do that to intimidate and to force you to make a mistake.

Say. "**I do not understand**" over an over again, **regardless** of the question.

IF YOU DO NOT UNDERSTAND A QUESTION, DO NOT ANSWER IT. Say, "**I do not understand**".

In fact, you can say this **to any question** the judge asks, such as what is your name.

Court tricks... They sometimes **start offering plea bargains**. The only way they can get you is **to scare you into a plea**.

Without **jurisdiction** (your permission) **they have to let you go**.

I have seen this work in courts **100%** of the time, but there can always be an exception.

When you say "**I do not understand**", the judge will ask you leading questions like, "**Do you understand English**? Can you **read English**? and etc... If you answer yes, then **he can assume that you DO understand**.

Simply say, "**No, I do not understand**". The Judge may say, "You answered me in English, you do understand." Say, "**I do not understand**".

"**I do not understand**" is a great way to answer **everything,** after you tell him you are the **beneficiary**.

And for the nervous types who cannot think under pressure, it is the best way to answer **at all times, places and circumstances**.

Rarely do folks get this hard of time, but **do prepare for it** just in case.

If you **stick to your guns** and **not take a plea bargain,** etc... charges have always been dismissed.

If you are ever arrested for anything in the future, **never give your name**. Say **you are not that 'person'** but are the **beneficiary and living soul**.

Used to be that they would **hold you for 72 hours and then let you go** if they could not **get you to say your name** or to take bail or bond.

But now **they can hold you up to ten days** and then offer you bail, bond, or "**Return of your own Recognizance**". This is a trick, **if you accept the offer**, you are then **giving them jurisdiction**.

They have to let you go, **sometime, after ten days** anyway.

"**I am not that person and it would be <u>bond fraud</u> for me to accept. Let me go**".

The judge will sometimes address you saying, "**Mr. Smith this and Mr. Smith that…**" If you answer to the name, then again **you are that person**. The judge just tricked you into **his jurisdiction**.

Simply say "**I don't know who you are talking to. I am not the 'person' Mr. Smith. I am the beneficiary and I gave you the 'person' per the birth certificate**".

NOTE:

If you ever noticed when someone files a lawsuit, **the court will dismiss the case saying that it is frivolous.** What they are saying is that *you cannot be the plaintiff because you are not the beneficiary.* So always **attach a copy** of your birth certificate to the suit.

"**All Rights Reserved**" — "**Without Prejudice**" — "**Without Prejudice per UCC 1-308**" — all lawful reservations.

"**Without Prejudice per UCC 1-308**", above or below your signature, **on an instrument,** represents the following:

• **It's not a promise to appear** and **eliminates perjury**.

• Enforces **the Right to contract** and the right to **compromise an unconscionable contract**.

• Reserves all applicable rights in **Bill of Rights** and **Article III judicial Power** under common law.

• **Criminal intent** must be brought forward to proceed.

• Upholds **Separation of Powers**.

• All terms **Constitutional** dealing with contracts, judicial and taxes.

• Reserves "**personam**" jurisdictional issues.

• Estoppel of subject matter jurisdiction, and summary Admiralty.

• Non-assumpsit.

• Habeas Corpus.

• Activating clause for police power at "**probable cause.**"

• Disrupts Penumbra Doctrine.

• Confession and avoidance.

Miranda will be given for you to sign. Reserve your rights on this instrument by not becoming **in personam** at Rule 12 (b). Do not give up your personam to "power of attorney" because you waive rights with each admission or tacit response answered by "persons standing in your stead," which makes you in personam for accepting this "benefit." Remain SILENT and the reservation will command you to Justice.

"**Without Prejudice UCC 1-308**" above or below your signature not only **puts a condition on an unconditional contract**, but also **reserves all your rights under Article III Judicial**.

Voids Police power unless "**crime**" and "**probable cause exist**".

"**An unconstitutional statute**, though having the form of law, **is in reality, no law** and imposes no duties, confers no rights, creates no office, bestows no power on anyone and justifies no actions performed under it." (**Am. Jur. 2d Sec. 256**).

The **graduated income tax**, for example, **is unconstitutional** only if the citizen **abates its 'color of law' — 'without Prejudice' to him**. (abate: **'put an end to its effect'**)

— — —

Without Prejudice serves notice upon any agent, that **you are not waiving any of your stated Bill of Rights**.

Beware of agency procedure and **sign everything** with **The reservation** to make the instrument "**non-assumpsit**". (free of liability).

Black's. **Non-assumpsit.** The general issue in the action of assumpsit; being a plea by which the defendant avers "**he did not partake" or promise as alleged**.

"But whenever the Judicial Power is called into play it is **responsible to the fundamental law** and no other authority can intervene to force or authorize the judicial body to disregard it." (**Yakus v. U.S. 321 U.S. 414 pg. 468 (1944)**).

The officer **may not know the Law** and will probably proceed with **whatever "forum" is to be taken** per his training instructions.

He is **a "ministerial" officer of the court** and is given very little discretional knowledge.

When our **Rights are violated** by agency, we must cooperate **with constitutional remedy and recourse**.

The agents **must sign forms also** and these become a **permanent record** of the administrative process that will receive **your judicial notice**.

Our **state citizenship** is brought forth along with our **personam Rights**, which do not mingle well with statute procedure.

The purpose of your **court appearance** would be **to gain jurisdiction** over your **personam**.

I would suggest that **for study purposes** that you **answer politely that you do not understand the charges** and "**without prejudice under Uniform Commercial Code 1-308, due to mistakes in fact and Law, I wish to remain silent**".

The magistrate will have to be **very constructive** in his color of law procedure **because his boundaries** to engage you further **are abated**.

Without **contract** or **tacit consent to the jurisdiction**, their claim is finished.

Remember, **you are in an Article I "inferior" court**, brought by Admiralty and **the only power this court has over the sovereign Citizen is to give Remedy** or **take the issue to the Grand Jury for indictment under Article III, if there is criminal intent**.

The 5th Amendment states; "No person shall be held to answer for a **capitol, or otherwise infamous crime**, unless on **presentment of a Grand Jury...**" If there is <u>no victim</u> and <u>criminal intent</u>, there is <u>no crime</u>.

"It may however, be **considered settled** that **letters or admissions containing the expression in substance** that they are to be "**without prejudice**" will not be **admitted in evidence**...an arrangement stating that the letter was **without prejudice** was held to be **inadmissible as evidence**... not only will the letter bearing the words, "**without prejudice**" but **also the answer thereto**, which was not so guarded, **was inadmissible**." (Ferry v. Taylor, 33 Mo. 323; Durgin v. Somers, 117 Mass 55, Molyneaux v. Collier, 13 Ga. 406).

When **We The People** are put into a **circumstance of compromise**, the only viable solution relies on **The Uniform Commercial Code** and its direct link to **The Constitution for these united States of America**.

<u>**Important**</u> : **UCC 1-207 was moved to UCC 1-308 — to hide it from the public.**

If all goes well, **you may be put on a red flag list**.
There appears to be **3 red flag lists**.

(1) **the judges list**, appears to be a **list of people** against whom the judge will not issue a **warrent for arrest** unless they cause injury — but the judge will still let the police ticket you or arrest you.

(2) **The state list**, is a **list of people** where there will not only be no arrest warrents, but where the police **cannot arrest you or ticket you or detain you** unless you are causing injury. YOU ARE ONLY PROTECTED **IN THE STATE** THAT HAS PUT YOU ON THEIR LIST. If you move to another state and change to the new state's ID, then you can get tickets and/or be arrested.

(3) **The federal list** is like the state list, except that **you are protected in all states and territories**. However, you can no longer get on this list **by sending a federal judge a letter of your reservation of rights**. You have to **sue your way** onto this list, and **possibly appeal**.

How UCC 1-308 works

The **US Constitution** establishes the **court's jurisdiction** as **common law**, **equity** and **admiralty** under **Article 3**.

As opposed to this...

The **Federal Corporation** establishes a **similar** jurisdiction except under the **Uniform Commercial Code**.

See **UCC 1-103. Supplementary General Principles of Law Applicable**.

Unless displaced by the particular provisions of this Act, *the principles of law and equity,* including the law merchant and the law relative to capacity to contract, principal and agent, estoppel, fraud, misrepresentation, duress, coercion, mistake, Bankruptcy, or other validating or invalidating cause *shall supplement its provisions*.

Anytime you see **law by itself**, as in the foregoing, *it means the common law,* except that they are taking the common law jurisdiction from the contract UCC. *The remedy of course is UCC 1-308.* So *the UCC is a deceptive criminal contractual constitution (of sorts)* to those who use it against us.

UCC 1-308 is the **Remedy** for any legal process **under commercial law** in the **United States.**

• **UCC § 1-308. Performance or Acceptance Under Reservation of Rights**. (a) A party that with explicit **reservation of rights** performs or promises performance or assents to performance in a manner demanded or offered by the other party **does not thereby prejudice the rights reserved**. Such words as "**without prejudice**" - "**under protest**" - or the like - **are sufficient**.

• Since the **Federal Corporation** is just that, **a corporation**. It has no jurisdiction **except with those that contract with it**. Also see **Congressional act of 1871** and **28 USC 3002**, Part VI, chapter 176, sub chapter 176, subsection A, (15) "**United States**" means **a Federal corporation**...

The states **illegally contracted** with the **Federal corporation** by passing the **Uniform Commercial Code** making themselves as well as the unsuspecting people **subject to the Federal corporation** and also **to the states** in their new commercial capacities.

• The **Uniform Commercial Code** creates the **corporate State of the United States**, the Federal corporation, as opposed to **the several dejure States of the union**. (UCC 1-201. General Definitions. (38) "**State**" means **State of the United States**...

As opposed to **the several states of the union**...
USC TITLE 28 > PART VI > CHAPTER 176 > SUBCHAPTER A > § 3002 Definitions (14) "**State**" means **any of the several States**...

• Because **the states** accepted and passed the **Uniform Commercial Code**, they converted **state Citizens** into "**persons**" (legal entities / articles of commerce) and the **States** into **vessels of the United States** placing the **States** and **state Citizens** under **maritime law**. (See the brilliant *word smithing* in the following).

USC TITLE 18 > PART I > CHAPTER 1 > § 9. Vessel of the United States defined
The term "**vessel of the United States**", as used in this title, means a **vessel belonging in whole or in part to the United States**, or any **citizen thereof**, or any **corporation created by or under the laws of the United States**, or of any **State, Territory, District, or possession thereof**.

Therefore **all laws** (color of law) **are contractual commercial laws** and the **remedy is UCC 1-308**. The Uniform Commercial Code **makes all crimes commercial only by contract** as per **27 CFR 72.11**. The problem is that **only the higher courts** will recognize **the remedy**. However, **the remedy should legally and always be give without delay - on demand or claim**. This of course is the problem. **The misdemeanor courts do not have a clue as to where their jurisdiction comes from** and **neither do magistrates**. You have to get in front of **a court with a real judge** that tries **felonies**. The courts try to string you along **under**

duress of threat hoping that you can be **scared into a plea**. But in the end **they have to honor the remedy**.

27 CFR 72.11 DISPOSITION OF SEIZED PERSONAL PROPERTY — Table of Contents

Subpart B **Definitions Commercial crimes. Any of the following types of crimes (Federal or State):** Offenses against the revenue laws; burglary; counterfeiting; forgery; kidnapping; larceny; robbery; illegal sale or possession of deadly weapons; prostitution (*including soliciting, procuring, pandering, white slaving, keeping house of ill fame, and like offenses*); extortion; swindling and confidence games; **and attempting to commit, conspiring to commit, or compounding any of the foregoing crimes**. Addiction to narcotic drugs and use of marihuana will be treated as if such were **commercial** crime.

<u>1938</u> - April 25 - The Supreme Court **overturned the standing precedents of the prior 150 years concerning "COMMON LAW" in the federal government**. (*Because there is no longer silver or gold coin as article one section 10 of the constitution.*)

"THERE IS NO FEDERAL COMMON LAW, AND CONGRESS HAS NO POWER TO DECLARE SUBSTANTIVE RULES OF COMMON LAW **applicable** IN A STATE, WHETHER **they be** LOCAL **or** GENERAL **in their nature, be they** COMMERCIAL LAW **or a part of** LAW OF TORTS". **(Erie Railroad Co. v. Thomkins, 304 U.S. 64, 82 L. Ed. 1188)**.

The **Common Law** is the **fountain source** of **Substantive and Remedial Rights**, if not **our very Liberties**. The members and associates of **The BAR** thereafter formed committees and granted themselves **special privileges, immunities and franchises**, and held meetings concerning **Judicial procedures**, and further, **to amend laws "to conform to a trend of judicial decisions** or to **accomplish similar objectives"**, including hodge-podging **the jurisdictions of Law and Equity together**, which is known today as "**One Form of Action**".

(See Constitution and By Laws, Article 3, Section 3.3(c), 1990-91 Reference Book, also Colorado Methods of Practice, West Publishing, Vol. 4, pages 2-3, Authors Comments.)

1939 - **ABA** (American BAR Association) gets more involved in **approval of uniform law products**. Thirty-nine acts are presented to the **Board of Governors of the ABA** for consideration and approval. During the same year, **all acts on aeronautics and motor vehicles are eliminated** as well as the **Land Registration Act, Child Labor Act of 1930, Uniform Divorce Jurisdiction Act, Firearms Act, Marriage Act** and more. **Six acts *are reclassified* as Model acts**.

1940 - At start of the decade, after deletions, etc., **53 acts out of 93** which had been approved since the group's founding **remain on the books**. Drafting committee for the Uniform Commercial Code (UCC) approved.

1941 - Speaking of the **Commercial Code project**, the Conference president states: "....this is the most important and the most far reaching project on which the conference has ever embarked." **It would take the major part of the next 10 year period to complete**.

1942 - **UCC effort begins in earnest** with completion of work on the revised **Uniform Sales Act**.

1943 - Members of the conference participate in **the drafting committee** in Washington, D.C. to work on **legislation which the government might desire** in connection with the **war effort**. No new acts.

1944 - Conference receives $150,000 grant from the **Falk Foundation** of Pittsburgh **to support work on the UCC**.

1945 - No annual meeting for the first time due to **difficulties of civilian transport** during the war.

1946 - **Falk Foundation increases its support** of the UCC with an additional $100,000.

1947 - **Uniform Law Conference** (ULC) and **American Law Institute** (ALI) join in partnership to put all the components together for the UCC. **Uniform Divorce Recognition Act** approved.

1950 - Approval of the **Uniform Marriage License Application Act, Uniform Adoption Act** and the **Uniform Reciprocal Enforcement of Support Act** (URESA). The latter has been one of the most successful ULC products.

1951 - May 18 - **During a joint meeting** with the **American Law Institute** in Washington, D.C., **the UCC was approved.** Later that year **the ABA formally approved the code as well.** Considered the outstanding accomplishment of the Conference, **the Code remains the ULC's signature product**.

As one of the **Uniform Laws** drafted by the **National Conference of Commissioners on Uniform State Laws** and the **American Law Institute** governing **commercial transactions** (including sales and leasing of goods, transfer of funds, commercial paper, bank deposits and collections, letters of credit, bulk transfers, warehouse receipts, bills of lading, investment securities, and secured transactions), **The Uniform Commercial Code (UCC) has been adopted in whole or substantially by all states**. (See: Blacks Law, 6th Ed. pg. 1531) In essence, **all court decisions are based on commercial law or business law** with **criminal penalties** associated with it. Rather than openly calling this new law **Admiralty/Maritime Jurisdiction**, it is called **Statutory Jurisdiction**.

America is a bankrupt nation owned completely by its creditors !

The creditors **own the Congress**, they **own the Executive**, they **own the Judiciary** and they **own all the State governments**. Do you have a Birth Certificate? They own you too.

Last note: **The 14th amendment creates a lower class of citizen - "citizen of the United States" -** rather than **the higher** class of citizen - "**Citizen of one of the several states of the union**". The **remedy** provided to the 14th amendment, is an **act by congress** known as **15 U.S. Statute at Large**, July 27, 1868 - **one day before the 14th Amendment took effect** - also known as the "**Expatriation Statute**". This is **your remedy** to claim to being a **natural Citizen of your state**. This makes you a **higher Citizen** and no longer subject to the **Article 4 loophole** that deprives you of your rights.

(Gone is the self-evident truth "**that all men are created equal**...")

The **Uniform Commercial Code** is **Private International Law** that is owned by **UNIDROIT**.

Does the UCC apply to you?

"...the body of learning we call *conflict of laws* is called *private international law* because it pertains to **private interests**, while *public international law* pertains to **relations between states**."

(Garner v. Teamsters, Chauffeurs& Helpers Local Union, 346 US 485, 495; 98 L Ed 228; 74 S Ct 161).

"In the sense of *public international law*, the **several states of the Union** are **not foreign to the United States** nor are they **foreign to each other**, but such is not the case in the field of *private international law*."

(Robinson v. Norato, 71 RI 256, 43 A2d467, 162 ALR 362).

The Uniform Commercial Code, by the copyright owner's own admission, *is private international Law*.

In other words *the 50 united States of the Union are <u>publicly</u> united with each other* while <u>*privately*</u> *foreign to the United States*.

In other words, *private international law pertians to <u>private</u> interests* and *public international law pertains to <u>public</u> relations between states*.

To simplify the events that cause the confusion of *"Public is Private"* and *"Private is Public"* we include the following...

The first "**connection**" from the highest, potent position is that:

a. **77 Stat. 630-631, P.L. 88-243 (1963)** and **P.L. 88-244 (1963)** make the **Uniform Commercial Code** (UCC) **Private Law** for the municipal **District of Columbia** and the **federal United States**.

These **statutory laws/actions** expressly effect **citizens of the federal government**.

77 Stat. 630-631, P.L. 88-243 is "an **Act** that enacts the **Uniform Commercial Code** for the **District of Columbia, and for other purposes**".

This is where **the UCC functions** as the "**law of the land**" for the **Federal Government** (District of Columbia & Territories).

For sake of simplicity, "**Public Law**" (**P.L. 88-244**) is "**Private Law**" for **private corporate citizens**, and not for "**the people**".

(**i**) A **private law** is confined to particular individuals, associations, or corporations. (**50 AmJur 12, p.28**).

(**ii**) A **private law** can be enforced by a court of competent jurisdiction when statutes for its enforcement are enacted. (**20AmJur 33, pgs. 58, 59**).

(**iii**) Statutes creating corporations are **private** acts. (**20 AmJur 35, p.60**).

(**iv**) In this connection, **the Federal Reserve Act is private law**. Federal Reserve banks **derive their existence** and **corporatepower** from the **Federal Reserve Act**. (Armano v. Federal Reserve Bank 468 F.Supp 674 (1979)).

(**v**) The **distinction** between **public** acts and **private** acts is not always sharply defined **when published statutes are printed in their final form**. (Case v. Kelly 133 U.S. 21 (1890)).

b. It is all **private** law and **International Law** (but, may be referred to as **Private International Law**), and it is owned by the same people that own **public** law 88-243 (1968).

The UCC was written and is owned by UNIDROIT (International Institute for the Unification of PrivateLaw,

which is located **within the Vatican** about one hundred yards from the "**Holy See**", and...

(i) To properly address "**public law**" one must understand that a "**Private Corporate Charter**" owns "**public law**" and "**public law**" is "**statutory**".

Public Law was converted to **Public Policy** in 1938. (*policy = political = police*).

All **private corporations** (fictions), including governments, are under "**public policy**" and can only deal with **other corporations** (fictions).

(ii) **Private Man** is not affected by **public law, private law, or public policy,** as long as **Private Man** does not harm another **Private Man**. **He** is not "**statutory**", but "**lawful**".

(iii) **Public** means of, concerning, or affecting the **common unity of the people**, the **Assemblage of Private Man**.

(iv) **Private means** not available for public use, control, or participation — belonging to a particular person or persons, **as opposed to the public or the government** (remember, as a corporation, **the government becomes no more than any other corporate "person"**), not holding an official or public position.

(v) "The **entire taxing and monetary systems** are, hereby, placed **under the UCC**". (The Federal Tax Lien Act of 1966).

c. **The U.S.** pays **$260,000** per year to **UNIDROIT** for the use of the **copyrighted UCC**. The **International Registry** is the private law of **UNIDROIT**, and since the **United States** has signed onto the **UNIDROIT** statute (**the International Institute for the Unification of PrivateLaw**), all of which is incorporated herein by reference in its entirety, which is all about **Private International Law**, which is another name for the **Uniform Commercial Code**.

On Page 6, "Legislative Activities", the the first item is "**Principles of International Commercial Contracts**", and on page 10 it shows; "**1955 Benelux Treaty on Compulsory Insurance against Civil Liability in respect of Motor**

Vehicles", and "**1958 Convention concerning the recognition and enforcement of decisions relating to maintenance obligations towards children**" (Hague Conference on Private International Law).

UNIDROIT is owned and operated by the **Vatican**, and they intend to enforce their *religious ceremony* on the millions of people on the land in America and elsewhere in the world. This is further proof that the **corporation called United States** is owned and operated by the **Vatican** to further their agenda, and they are using their **commercial law** to enforce their **martial law**.

No law compels a **private-sector non-governmentally-privileged work-eligible woman or man** to submit a **W-4 or W-9 form** (or their equivalents), nor to obtain or disclose a **SSN** as a condition of **being hired** or of **keeping his job**.

With the **exception of an order** from a court of competent jurisdiction issued by a duly qualified judge, **no amounts can be lawfully taken from one's pay** (for taxes, fees or other charges) **without the worker's explicit, intentional, knowing, voluntary, written consent**.

*"It is the manner of enforcement which gives **Title 42 1983** its unique importance, for **enforcement is placed in the hands of the people**. Each citizen acts as a **private attorney general** who '**takes on the mantel of the sovereign**' guarding for all of us the individual liberties enunciated in the Constitution"* (Frankenhauser v. Rizzo, 59 F.R.D. (1973).

SECTION IX. — Assassination.

148. *The law of war does not allow proclaiming either an individual belonging to the hostile army, or a citizen, or a subject of the hostile government **an outlaw, who may be slain without trial by any captor,** any more than the modern law of peace **allows such international outlawry;** on the contrary, it abhors such outrage. The sternest retaliation should follow the murder committed in consequence of such proclamation, made by whatever authority. **Civilized nations***

look with horror upon offers of rewards for the assassination of enemies as relapses into barbarism.

"The laws of congress in respect to those matters do not extend into the territorial limits of the states, but have force only in the District of Columbia, and other places that are within the exclusive jurisdiction of the national government."
CAHA v. U.S., 152 U.S. 211 (1894)

UNDER THE LAWS OF COMMERCE TRUTH IS SOVEREIGN

The foundation of the Uniform Commercial Code (UCC) is Commercial Law.

The foundation of Commercial Law is based upon certain universal, eternally just, valid, moral precepts and truths. The basis of Commercial Law is the Law of Exodus of the Old Testament (i.e. The 10 Commandments), and the Judaic Orthodox Hebrew Commercial law of Moses.

The Laws of Commerce, unchanged for at least six thousand years, form the basis of western civilization, if not all nations of the world. Therefore Commercial Law applies universally throughout the world.

Commercial Law is non-judicial. It is prior to, superior to, and the basis of [and cannot be set aside or overruled by] the statutes of any government, legislature, governmental, or quasi-governmental, agencies, courts, judges, and law enforcement agencies, all of which are under an inherent obligation to uphold said Commercial Law.

Commercial Law is a "War of Truth" expressed in the form of an intellectual weapon called an *Affidavit*.

An Affidavit is simply a written list of facts, or truths, signed under the penalty of perjury, and usually notarized. The person making and signing an affidavit is called the *"affiant"*. It is "survival of the fittest" where the last unrebutted affidavit stands triumphant as the truth.

The UCC Connection

THE 10 MAXIMS
OF COMMERCIAL LAW

1. "A workman is worthy of his hire." — Exodus 20:15; Lev. 19:13; Matt. 10:10; Luke 10:7; II Tim. 2:6. (*"It is against equity for freemen not to have the free disposal of their own property."*);

2. "All are equal under the law." — Exodus 21:23-25; Lev. 24:17-21; Deut. 1:17, 19:21; Matt. 22:36-40; Luke 10:17; Col. 3:25. (*"No one is above the law.";* *"Commerce, by the law of nations, ought to be common, and not be converted into a monopoly for the private gain of a few."*);

3. "In commerce, truth is sovereign." — Exodus 20:16; Psalm 117:2; John 8:32; II Cor. 13:8. (*"To lie is to go against the mind.";* *Oriental proverb: "Of all that is good, sublimity is supreme."*);

4. "Truth is expressed in the form of an affidavit." — Lev. 5:4-5; Lev. 6:3-5; Lev. 19:11-13; Num. 30:2; Matt. 5:33; James 5:12.

5. "An unrebutted affidavit stands as truth in commerce." — 1 Pet. 1:25; Heb. 6:13-15. (*"He who does not deny, admits."*);

6. "An unrebutted affidavit becomes judgment in commerce." — Heb. 6:16-17. (*Any proceeding in court, tribunal, or arbitration forum consists of a contest or "duel" of commercial affidavits wherein the remaining points not rebutted in the end stand as the truth of the matters to which the judgment of law is applied.*)

7. "A matter must be expressed to be resolved." — Heb 4:16; Phil 4:5; Eph 6:19-21. (*"He who fails to assert his rights has none."*);

8. "He who leaves the field of battle first (does not respond to the Affidavit) **loses by default."** — Job; Matt 10:22. (*"He who does not repel a wrong when he can, occasions it."*);

9. "Sacrifice is the measure of credibility." — Acts 7, life/death of Stephen. (*"He who bears the burden ought to derive the benefit."*) — One who is not damaged, put at risk, or willing to swear an oath on his commercial liability, for the truth of his statements, and the legitimacy of his actions, has no basis to assert charges or claims, and forfeits all credibility and right to authority.

10. "A lien or claim can be satisfied only through (a) rebuttal by counter affidavit point by point; (b) resolution by a jury; or (c) payment or performance of the claim." — Gen. 2-3; Matt 4; Revelation. (*"If the plaintiff fails to prove his case, the defendant is absolved."*)

Because Truth is sovereign in commerce, and everyone is responsible for propagating the truth in all their speaking, writing, and acting, all commercial processes function by affidavits, certified under oath to be "true, correct, not misleading, and complete," on each affiant's commercial liability regarding all matters stated and likewise demanded.

In written matters — on nearly every document that those who run the System desire that you sign — your signature is presumed to be under penalty of perjury.

In a court setting, however, testimony (an oral commercial affidavit) is sworn to be "the truth, the whole truth, and nothing but the truth, so help me God." The participant must provide material evidence — i.e. ledgering/bookkeeping — proving that each fact or entry is true, valid, verifiable and relevant.

Without the acceptance of liability in support of one's assertions, no credibility is established.

44694179R00039